CONTENTS

Meet Camila and her family

Papá

Mamá

Ana, age 14

Andres, age 10

Camila, age 7

Spanish glossary

domingo allowance

gané I won

me rindo I give up

torneo tournament, contest

Camila's family is originally from Mexico. They sometimes speak Spanish at home.

Chapter 1

THE GOAL

"I need a camera, a stand and a microphone," said Camila.

"For what?" asked Papá.

"For my WeTube channel," said Camila.

"You should save your **domingo**," said Papá.

Camila sighed.

It would take forever to save up enough money.

"There is a video game **torneo** next month," said her brother, Andres. "The prize is two hundred pounds."

Camila perked up.

"That is more than enough to buy what I need!" she said.

Then her shoulders sank.

"I don't know how to play video games," she said.

"I have an old laptop you can use to learn," said Papá.

"I have a controller you can use with the laptop," said Andres.

"I have a membership to StreamHouse," said Ana. "You can play some games for free."

Chapter 2

THE CHALLENGE

Camila started playing the next day after school.

A minute after she began, Camila lost.

"Game Over," said the computer.

She wrinkled her nose. "I can do better than that," she said.

She tried again.

"Game Over," it said again.

"Game Over."

"Game Over."

"Come on," said Camila.
She pushed up her sleeves
and hit *Start*.

"No game will defeat me!"
she said. "I'll be the best gamer
in the world by next month."

She wandered into a magical forest and then . . . Game Over.

GAME OVER

"I'll be the best gamer in the whole city," she said, mostly sure of herself.

She wobbled on the edge of a blazing volcano and then . . . Game Over.

After three weeks, Camila put down the controller. She walked into the living room. Her family was watching a film.

"**Me rindo**," said Camila. She sank into the sofa. "I'll never be a real gamer."

"You've still got a week until the **torneo**," said Papá. "Are you sure you want to give up?"

"I can't stand it any more," said Camila. "I dream about trolls. I dream about battles."

"Maybe your brain is practising," said Andres.

"But I keep losing in my dream," said Camila. "I just want to read a book."

"Maybe taking a break will help you decide," said Mamá.

Chapter 3
WIN OR LOSE

Camila picked up her favourite book, *The Secret Garden*. She read it all weekend.

She dreamt of seeds and robins and hundreds of flowers.

In between reading, she went to the market with her parents. She played with her cat, Pancho. She went to the park.

On Monday morning, she felt rested and refreshed. But she still didn't know what to do about the tournament.

On Monday afternoon, Papá got an email from the **torneo** leaders.

"It says you need to be at the gaming room by 10:00 a.m. on Saturday," said Papá.

"Do you still want to give up?" said Mamá.

Camila bit her lip. How could she be a star if she kept losing?

She didn't care about the money anymore. She cared about doing the right thing.

She wanted to do what a star would do.

A star wouldn't quit just because something was hard.

She stood up straight. "I'm going to do it," she said.

She started up her laptop.

She faced a
monster and . . .
Game Over.

She battled
a giant and . . .
Game Over.

A dragon
charged her
shield and . . .

Victory!

"**¡Gané! ¡Gané!**" she ran to tell her family.

"Whoop! Whoop!" they said and gave her high fives.

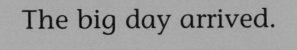

The big day arrived.

Camila sat in front of a

gaming system. She worked

hard.

Her avatar dodged and struck
and jumped and flipped.

But . . . "Game Over."

Camila didn't win the prize money. But she saved her allowance.

And in six months . . .

"Welcome to my WeTube Channel," she said to her video camera. "My first topic is 'How to be a video game star, even if you lose.'"

Design a video game monster!

Camila faced scary beasts in her video game. Imagine you are a video game designer, and your job is to come up with a dangerous monster for a new video game.

WHAT YOU NEED
- white paper
- several colours of paint
- googly eyes
- glue
- felt-tips
- feathers, buttons, glitter or other decorations (optional)

WHAT YOU DO

1. Fold one sheet of paper in half, then open it and lay it flat. Squirt different colours of paint on one side of the crease.

2. Refold the paper and squash the sides together. Open it to see your monster shape. Let it dry.

3. When dry, add any details you want to your monster. How many eyes does your monster have? Do you need to draw arms, legs or other body parts? Add other decorations if you want.

4. On a separate piece of paper, write some details about your monster's personality. Make sure you give your monster a name and list its strengths and weaknesses.

Glossary

allowance   an amount of money given regularly for a specific purpose

avatar   a character made to stand in for a person on a video game

controller   a piece of equipment used to control the actions on a video game

microphone   an instrument used to capture sound waves so they can be recorded

victory   a win in a game or contest

volcano   a mountain with vents through which molten lava, ash and gas may erupt

Think about the story

1. Camila entered the video game tournament for the prize money. She did not want to save up her allowance for the equipment she wanted. Is it hard to save money for something big? Why or why not?

2. In which ways did Camila's family help her get ready for the video game tournament?

3. Do you think Camila was playing video games too much? Explain your answer.

4. Were you surprised about the ending of the story? Why or why not?

About the author

Alicia Salazar is a Mexican American children's book author who has written for blogs, magazines and educational publishers. She was also once a primary school teacher and a marine biologist. She currently lives in the suburbs of Houston, Texas, USA, but is a city girl at heart. When Alicia is not dreaming up new adventures to experience, she is turning her adventures into stories for kids.

About the illustrator

Thais Damião is a Brazilian illustrator and graphic designer. Born and raised in a small city in Rio de Janeiro State, Brazil, she spent her childhood playing with her brother and cousins and drawing all the time. Her illustrations are dedicated to children and inspired by nature and friendship. Thais currently lives in California, USA.